# SACRED STORY YOUTH

# FOURTH GRADE

## MY MEDITATION RESPONSE BOOK

Illustration by Léopold Marboeuf

# SACRED STORY PRESS

1401 E Jefferson St., STE 405

Seattle, WA 981222

All rights reserved. No part of this book shall be reproduced, stored in a retrieval system, or transmitted by any means - electronic, mechanical, photocopying, recording, or otherwise - without written permission from the publisher. The only exception is brief quotations in printed reviews. Although every precaution has been taken in the preparation of this book, the publisher and author assume no responsibility for errors or omissions. Neither is any liability assumed for damages resulting from the use of the information contained herein.

Copyright © 2015 Sacred Story Press

All rights reserved.

ISBN-13: 978-1514332986

ISBN-10: 1514332981

We are also exceedingly pleased to be reintroducing back to the world the extraordinary art of Léopold Marboeuf (1916-2006) in the *My Sacred Story Missal* and the *Sacred Story Youth Meditation Response Logs*. Printing of the Missal and images was granted by Templegate Publishers, Springfield, Illinois.

# Dedicated to Our Lady of the Way

Dear Friend of Christ Jesus:

This is your personal Sacred Story Youth response log book. You are invited to listen to the daily meditations. The SACRED STORY YOUTH meditation quiets your mind so you can hear the voice of God in your heart. Find a safe and sacred place to keep this response log.

After listening you can write one word or short phrase or draw a joy or sadness that you experienced during your meditation time. Here is a sample of each!

**CONSOLATION:** "Family visiting time"

**DESOLATION:** "When I don't get along with my sister"

Remember to review your words each week so you can begin to "see" how the different spirits are at work in your life. The more you review your words, the more you will learn about God, yourself and what will lead you to happiness and peace.

Sincerely,

Fr. Bill Watson, S.J.

President, President/Founder
Sacred Story Institute

# DIRECTIONS

1.  Listen to daily meditation.

2.  After listening to the daily meditation take one minute to draw or write a word or short phrase to a Consolation and Desolation that surfaced in your day's meditation.   Let your heart write for you...it doesn't have to be perfect, but rather your word, phrase or picture should capture as best you can the feeling of spiritual consolation (increase of faith, hope and love) or spiritual desolation (a decrease of faith, hope or love).
Last year and the year before, you were asked to write words that made you happy or sad. Now you are old enough to understand that what makes you happy and sad are spiritual realities we call consolation and desolation.

Consolations are spiritual movements in your soul that increase your joy, hope, and faith.

Desolations are spiritual movements in your soul  that decrease your joy, hope and faith.

You are a spiritual being and God gave you spiritual radar as a gift to sense what is good and bad for you by listening to these consolations and desolations. Simple!

# ETERNITY

I believe God loved me into life and so I commit myself never to break relationship with anyone by taking from them what does not belong to me or even desire to do so!

| WEEK _____ | Write one word or phrase that brought you consolation today. Keep in mind joy because you are alive and loved - not because of "things" you possessed or did not possess. | OR: Write one word or phrase that brought you desolation today. Keep in mind sadness when you might have linked your self-worth to "things" you possessed or did not possess. |
|---|---|---|
| MONDAY | | |
| TUESDAY | | |
| WEDNESDAY | | |
| THURSDAY | | |
| FRIDAY | | |

| | | |
|---|---|---|
| THE WEEK'S MOST SIGNIFICANT CONSOLATION | | |
| THE WEEK'S MOST SIGNIFICANT DESOLATION | | |
| THE MOST IMPORTANT THING YOU LEARNED THIS WEEK | | |

# ETERNITY

I believe God loved me into life and so I commit myself never to break relationship with anyone by taking from them what does not belong to me or even desire to do so!

| WEEK _____ | Write one word or phrase that brought you consolation today. Keep in mind joy because you are alive and loved - not because of "things" you possessed or did not possess. | OR: Write one word or phrase that brought you desolation today. Keep in mind sadness when you might have linked your self-worth to "things" you possessed or did not possess. |
|---|---|---|
| MONDAY | | |
| TUESDAY | | |
| WEDNESDAY | | |
| THURSDAY | | |
| FRIDAY | | |

| | | |
|---|---|---|
| <br>**THE WEEK'S MOST SIGNIFICANT CONSOLATION** | | |
| <br>**THE WEEK'S MOST SIGNIFICANT DESOLATION** | | |
| <br>**THE MOST IMPORTANT THING YOU LEARNED THIS WEEK** | | |

# ETERNITY

I believe God loved me into life and so I commit myself never to break relationship with anyone by taking from them what does not belong to me or even desire to do so!

| WEEK _____ | Write one word or phrase that brought you consolation today. Keep in mind joy because you are alive and loved – not because of "things" you possessed or did not possess. | OR: Write one word or phrase that brought you desolation today. Keep in mind sadness when you might have linked your self-worth to "things" you possessed or did not possess. |
|---|---|---|
| MONDAY | | |
| TUESDAY | | |
| WEDNESDAY | | |
| THURSDAY | | |
| FRIDAY | | |

THE WEEK'S
MOST
SIGNIFICANT
CONSOLATION

THE WEEK'S
MOST
SIGNIFICANT
DESOLATION

THE MOST
IMPORTANT
THING YOU
LEARNED THIS
WEEK

# ETERNITY

I believe God loved me into life and so I commit myself never to break relationship with anyone by taking from them what does not belong to me or even desire to do so!

| WEEK _____ | Write one word or phrase that brought you consolation today. Keep in mind joy because you are alive and loved - not because of "things" you possessed or did not possess. | OR: Write one word or phrase that brought you desolation today. Keep in mind sadness when you might have linked your self-worth to "things" you possessed or did not possess. |
|---|---|---|
| MONDAY | | |
| TUESDAY | | |
| WEDNESDAY | | |
| THURSDAY | | |
| FRIDAY | | |

| | | |
|---|---|---|
| THE WEEK'S MOST SIGNIFICANT CONSOLATION | | |
| THE WEEK'S MOST SIGNIFICANT DESOLATION | | |
| THE MOST IMPORTANT THING YOU LEARNED THIS WEEK | | |

# ETERNITY

I believe God loved me into life and so I commit myself never to break relationship with anyone by taking from them what does not belong to me or even desire to do so!

| WEEK _____ | Write one word or phrase that brought you consolation today. Keep in mind joy because you are alive and loved - not because of "things" you possessed or did not possess. | OR: Write one word or phrase that brought you desolation today. Keep in mind sadness when you might have linked your self-worth to "things" you possessed or did not possess. |
|---|---|---|
| MONDAY | | |
| TUESDAY | | |
| WEDNESDAY | | |
| THURSDAY | | |
| FRIDAY | | |

| | | |
|---|---|---|
| **THE WEEK'S MOST SIGNIFICANT CONSOLATION** | | |
| **THE WEEK'S MOST SIGNIFICANT DESOLATION** | | |
| **THE MOST IMPORTANT THING YOU LEARNED THIS WEEK** | | |

# ETERNITY

I believe God loved me into life and so I commit myself never to break relationship with anyone by taking from them what does not belong to me or even desire to do so!

| WEEK _____ | Write one word or phrase that brought you consolation today. Keep in mind joy because you are alive and loved - not because of "things" you possessed or did not possess. | OR: Write one word or phrase that brought you desolation today. Keep in mind sadness when you might have linked your self-worth to "things" you possessed or did not possess. |
|---|---|---|
| MONDAY | | |
| TUESDAY | | |
| WEDNESDAY | | |
| THURSDAY | | |
| FRIDAY | | |

| | | |
|---|---|---|
| THE WEEK'S MOST SIGNIFICANT CONSOLATION | | |
| THE WEEK'S MOST SIGNIFICANT DESOLATION | | |
| THE MOST IMPORTANT THING YOU LEARNED THIS WEEK | | |

# ETERNITY

I believe God loved me into life and so I commit myself never to break relationship with anyone by taking from them what does not belong to me or even desire to do so!

| WEEK _____ | Write one word or phrase that brought you consolation today. Keep in mind joy because you are alive and loved<br>- not because of "things" you possessed or did not possess. | OR: Write one word or phrase that brought you desolation today. Keep in mind sadness when you might have linked your self-worth to "things" you possessed or did not possess. |
|---|---|---|
| MONDAY | | |
| TUESDAY | | |
| WEDNESDAY | | |
| THURSDAY | | |
| FRIDAY | | |

| | | |
|---|---|---|
| **THE WEEK'S MOST SIGNIFICANT CONSOLATION** | | |
| **THE WEEK'S MOST SIGNIFICANT DESOLATION** | | |
| **THE MOST IMPORTANT THING YOU LEARNED THIS WEEK** | | |

# ETERNITY

I believe God loved me into life and so I commit myself never to break relationship with anyone by taking from them what does not belong to me or even desire to do so!

| WEEK _____ | Write one word or phrase that brought you consolation today. Keep in mind joy because you are alive and loved - not because of "things" you possessed or did not possess. | OR: Write one word or phrase that brought you desolation today. Keep in mind sadness when you might have linked your self-worth to "things" you possessed or did not possess. |
|---|---|---|
| MONDAY | | |
| TUESDAY | | |
| WEDNESDAY | | |
| THURSDAY | | |
| FRIDAY | | |

| | | |
|---|---|---|
| THE WEEK'S MOST SIGNIFICANT CONSOLATION | | |
| THE WEEK'S MOST SIGNIFICANT DESOLATION | | |
| THE MOST IMPORTANT THING YOU LEARNED THIS WEEK | | |

# ETERNITY

I believe God loved me into life and so I commit myself never to break relationship with anyone by taking from them what does not belong to me or even desire to do so!

| WEEK _____ | Write one word or phrase that brought you consolation today. Keep in mind joy because you are alive and loved - not because of "things" you possessed or did not possess. | OR: Write one word or phrase that brought you desolation today. Keep in mind sadness when you might have linked your self-worth to "things" you possessed or did not possess. |
|---|---|---|
| MONDAY | | |
| TUESDAY | | |
| WEDNESDAY | | |
| THURSDAY | | |
| FRIDAY | | |

| | | |
|---|---|---|
| THE WEEK'S MOST SIGNIFICANT CONSOLATION | | |
| THE WEEK'S MOST SIGNIFICANT DESOLATION | | |
| THE MOST IMPORTANT THING YOU LEARNED THIS WEEK | | |

# ETERNITY

I believe God loved me into life and so I commit myself never to break relationship with anyone by taking from them what does not belong to me or even desire to do so!

| WEEK _____ | Write one word or phrase that brought you consolation today. Keep in mind joy because you are alive and loved<br>- not because of "things" you possessed or did not possess. | OR: Write one word or phrase that brought you desolation today. Keep in mind sadness when you might have linked your self-worth to "things" you possessed or did not possess. |
|---|---|---|
| MONDAY | | |
| TUESDAY | | |
| WEDNESDAY | | |
| THURSDAY | | |
| FRIDAY | | |

| | | |
|---|---|---|
| THE WEEK'S MOST SIGNIFICANT CONSOLATION | | |
| THE WEEK'S MOST SIGNIFICANT DESOLATION | | |
| THE MOST IMPORTANT THING YOU LEARNED THIS WEEK | | |

# ETERNITY

I believe God loved me into life and so I commit myself never to break relationship with anyone by taking from them what does not belong to me or even desire to do so!

| WEEK _____ | Write one word or phrase that brought you consolation today. Keep in mind joy because you are alive and loved - not because of "things" you possessed or did not possess. | OR: Write one word or phrase that brought you desolation today. Keep in mind sadness when you might have linked your self-worth to "things" you possessed or did not possess. |
|---|---|---|
| MONDAY | | |
| TUESDAY | | |
| WEDNESDAY | | |
| THURSDAY | | |
| FRIDAY | | |

| | | |
|---|---|---|
| THE WEEK'S MOST SIGNIFICANT CONSOLATION | | |
| THE WEEK'S MOST SIGNIFICANT DESOLATION | | |
| THE MOST IMPORTANT THING YOU LEARNED THIS WEEK | | |

# ETERNITY

I believe God loved me into life and so I commit myself never to break relationship with anyone by taking from them what does not belong to me or even desire to do so!

| WEEK _____ | Write one word or phrase that brought you consolation today. Keep in mind joy because you are alive and loved - not because of "things" you possessed or did not possess. | OR: Write one word or phrase that brought you desolation today. Keep in mind sadness when you might have linked your self-worth to "things" you possessed or did not possess. |
|---|---|---|
| MONDAY | | |
| TUESDAY | | |
| WEDNESDAY | | |
| THURSDAY | | |
| FRIDAY | | |

THE WEEK'S
MOST
SIGNIFICANT
CONSOLATION

THE WEEK'S
MOST
SIGNIFICANT
DESOLATION

THE MOST
IMPORTANT
THING YOU
LEARNED THIS
WEEK

# ETERNITY

I believe God loved me into life and so I commit myself never to break relationship with anyone by taking from them what does not belong to me or even desire to do so!

| WEEK _____ | Write one word or phrase that brought you consolation today. Keep in mind joy because you are alive and loved - not because of "things" you possessed or did not possess. | OR: Write one word or phrase that brought you desolation today. Keep in mind sadness when you might have linked your self-worth to "things" you possessed or did not possess. |
|---|---|---|
| MONDAY | | |
| TUESDAY | | |
| WEDNESDAY | | |
| THURSDAY | | |
| FRIDAY | | |

| THE WEEK'S MOST SIGNIFICANT CONSOLATION | | |
| --- | --- | --- |
| THE WEEK'S MOST SIGNIFICANT DESOLATION | | |
| THE MOST IMPORTANT THING YOU LEARNED THIS WEEK | | |

# ETERNITY

I believe God loved me into life and so I commit myself never to break relationship with anyone by taking from them what does not belong to me or even desire to do so!

| WEEK _____ | Write one word or phrase that brought you consolation today. Keep in mind joy because you are alive and loved - not because of "things" you possessed or did not possess. | OR: Write one word or phrase that brought you desolation today. Keep in mind sadness when you might have linked your self-worth to "things" you possessed or did not possess. |
|---|---|---|
| MONDAY | | |
| TUESDAY | | |
| WEDNESDAY | | |
| THURSDAY | | |
| FRIDAY | | |

|  | | |
|---|---|---|
| THE WEEK'S MOST SIGNIFICANT CONSOLATION | | |
| THE WEEK'S MOST SIGNIFICANT DESOLATION | | |
| THE MOST IMPORTANT THING YOU LEARNED THIS WEEK | | |

# ETERNITY

I believe God loved me into life and so I commit myself never to break relationship with anyone by taking from them what does not belong to me or even desire to do so!

| WEEK _____ | Write one word or phrase that brought you consolation today. Keep in mind joy because you are alive and loved - not because of "things" you possessed or did not possess. | OR: Write one word or phrase that brought you desolation today. Keep in mind sadness when you might have linked your self-worth to "things" you possessed or did not possess. |
| --- | --- | --- |
| MONDAY | | |
| TUESDAY | | |
| WEDNESDAY | | |
| THURSDAY | | |
| FRIDAY | | |

|  | | |
| --- | --- | --- |
| THE WEEK'S MOST SIGNIFICANT CONSOLATION | | |
| THE WEEK'S MOST SIGNIFICANT DESOLATION | | |
| THE MOST IMPORTANT THING YOU LEARNED THIS WEEK | | |

# ETERNITY

I believe God loved me into life and so I commit myself never to break relationship with anyone by taking from them what does not belong to me or even desire to do so!

| WEEK _____ | Write one word or phrase that brought you consolation today. Keep in mind joy because you are alive and loved<br>- not because of "things" you possessed or did not possess. | OR: Write one word or phrase that brought you desolation today. Keep in mind sadness when you might have linked your self-worth to "things" you possessed or did not possess. |
|---|---|---|
| MONDAY | | |
| TUESDAY | | |
| WEDNESDAY | | |
| THURSDAY | | |
| FRIDAY | | |

THE WEEK'S
MOST
SIGNIFICANT
CONSOLATION

THE WEEK'S
MOST
SIGNIFICANT
DESOLATION

THE MOST
IMPORTANT
THING YOU
LEARNED THIS
WEEK

# ETERNITY

I believe God loved me into life and so I commit myself never to break relationship with anyone by taking from them what does not belong to me or even desire to do so!

| WEEK _____ | Write one word or phrase that brought you consolation today. Keep in mind joy because you are alive and loved - not because of "things" you possessed or did not possess. | OR: Write one word or phrase that brought you desolation today. Keep in mind sadness when you might have linked your self-worth to "things" you possessed or did not possess. |
|---|---|---|
| MONDAY | | |
| TUESDAY | | |
| WEDNESDAY | | |
| THURSDAY | | |
| FRIDAY | | |

| | | |
|---|---|---|
| THE WEEK'S MOST SIGNIFICANT CONSOLATION | | |
| THE WEEK'S MOST SIGNIFICANT DESOLATION | | |
| THE MOST IMPORTANT THING YOU LEARNED THIS WEEK | | |

# ETERNITY

I believe God loved me into life and so I commit myself never to break relationship with anyone by taking from them what does not belong to me or even desire to do so!

| WEEK _____ | Write one word or phrase that brought you consolation today. Keep in mind joy because you are alive and loved<br>- not because of "things" you possessed or did not possess. | OR: Write one word or phrase that brought you desolation today. Keep in mind sadness when you might have linked your self-worth to "things" you possessed or did not possess. |
|---|---|---|
| MONDAY | | |
| TUESDAY | | |
| WEDNESDAY | | |
| THURSDAY | | |
| FRIDAY | | |

| **THE WEEK'S MOST SIGNIFICANT CONSOLATION** | | |
| --- | --- | --- |
| **THE WEEK'S MOST SIGNIFICANT DESOLATION** | | |
| **THE MOST IMPORTANT THING YOU LEARNED THIS WEEK** | | |

# ETERNITY

I believe God loved me into life and so I commit myself never to break relationship with anyone by taking from them what does not belong to me or even desire to do so!

| WEEK _____ | Write one word or phrase that brought you consolation today. Keep in mind joy because you are alive and loved - not because of "things" you possessed or did not possess. | OR: Write one word or phrase that brought you desolation today. Keep in mind sadness when you might have linked your self-worth to "things" you possessed or did not possess. |
| --- | --- | --- |
| MONDAY | | |
| TUESDAY | | |
| WEDNESDAY | | |
| THURSDAY | | |
| FRIDAY | | |

THE WEEK'S
MOST
SIGNIFICANT
CONSOLATION

THE WEEK'S
MOST
SIGNIFICANT
DESOLATION

THE MOST
IMPORTANT
THING YOU
LEARNED THIS
WEEK

# ETERNITY

I believe God loved me into life and so I commit myself never to break relationship with anyone by taking from them what does not belong to me or even desire to do so!

| WEEK _____ | Write one word or phrase that brought you consolation today. Keep in mind joy because you are alive and loved<br>- not because of "things" you possessed or did not possess. | OR: Write one word or phrase that brought you desolation today. Keep in mind sadness when you might have linked your self-worth to "things" you possessed or did not possess. |
| --- | --- | --- |
| MONDAY | | |
| TUESDAY | | |
| WEDNESDAY | | |
| THURSDAY | | |
| FRIDAY | | |

| THE WEEK'S MOST SIGNIFICANT CONSOLATION | | |
| --- | --- | --- |
| THE WEEK'S MOST SIGNIFICANT DESOLATION | | |
| THE MOST IMPORTANT THING YOU LEARNED THIS WEEK | | |

# ETERNITY

I believe God loved me into life and so I commit myself never to break relationship with anyone by taking from them what does not belong to me or even desire to do so!

| WEEK _____ | Write one word or phrase that brought you consolation today. Keep in mind joy because you are alive and loved - not because of "things" you possessed or did not possess. | OR: Write one word or phrase that brought you desolation today. Keep in mind sadness when you might have linked your self-worth to "things" you possessed or did not possess. |
|---|---|---|
| MONDAY | | |
| TUESDAY | | |
| WEDNESDAY | | |
| THURSDAY | | |
| FRIDAY | | |

| | | |
|---|---|---|
| THE WEEK'S MOST SIGNIFICANT CONSOLATION | | |
| THE WEEK'S MOST SIGNIFICANT DESOLATION | | |
| THE MOST IMPORTANT THING YOU LEARNED THIS WEEK | | |

# ETERNITY

I believe God loved me into life and so I commit myself never to break relationship with anyone by taking from them what does not belong to me or even desire to do so!

| WEEK _____ | Write one word or phrase that brought you consolation today. Keep in mind joy because you are alive and loved - not because of "things" you possessed or did not possess. | OR: Write one word or phrase that brought you desolation today. Keep in mind sadness when you might have linked your self-worth to "things" you possessed or did not possess. |
|---|---|---|
| MONDAY | | |
| TUESDAY | | |
| WEDNESDAY | | |
| THURSDAY | | |
| FRIDAY | | |

| | | |
|---|---|---|
| **THE WEEK'S MOST SIGNIFICANT CONSOLATION** | | |
| **THE WEEK'S MOST SIGNIFICANT DESOLATION** | | |
| **THE MOST IMPORTANT THING YOU LEARNED THIS WEEK** | | |

# ETERNITY

I believe God loved me into life and so I commit myself never to break relationship with anyone by taking from them what does not belong to me or even desire to do so!

| WEEK _____ | Write one word or phrase that brought you consolation today. Keep in mind joy because you are alive and loved - not because of "things" you possessed or did not possess. | OR: Write one word or phrase that brought you desolation today. Keep in mind sadness when you might have linked your self-worth to "things" you possessed or did not possess. |
| --- | --- | --- |
| MONDAY | | |
| TUESDAY | | |
| WEDNESDAY | | |
| THURSDAY | | |
| FRIDAY | | |

THE WEEK'S
MOST
SIGNIFICANT
CONSOLATION

THE WEEK'S
MOST
SIGNIFICANT
DESOLATION

THE MOST
IMPORTANT
THING YOU
LEARNED THIS
WEEK

# ETERNITY

I believe God loved me into life and so I commit myself never to break relationship with anyone by taking from them what does not belong to me or even desire to do so!

| WEEK _____ | Write one word or phrase that brought you consolation today. Keep in mind joy because you are alive and loved - not because of "things" you possessed or did not possess. | OR: Write one word or phrase that brought you desolation today. Keep in mind sadness when you might have linked your self-worth to "things" you possessed or did not possess. |
|---|---|---|
| MONDAY | | |
| TUESDAY | | |
| WEDNESDAY | | |
| THURSDAY | | |
| FRIDAY | | |

| <br>THE WEEK'S MOST SIGNIFICANT CONSOLATION | | |
| --- | --- | --- |
| <br>THE WEEK'S MOST SIGNIFICANT DESOLATION | | |
| <br>THE MOST IMPORTANT THING YOU LEARNED THIS WEEK | | |

# ETERNITY

I believe God loved me into life and so I commit myself never to break relationship with anyone by taking from them what does not belong to me or even desire to do so!

| WEEK _____ | Write one word or phrase that brought you consolation today. Keep in mind joy because you are alive and loved<br>- not because of "things" you possessed or did not possess. | OR: Write one word or phrase that brought you desolation today. Keep in mind sadness when you might have linked your self-worth to "things" you possessed or did not possess. |
|---|---|---|
| MONDAY | | |
| TUESDAY | | |
| WEDNESDAY | | |
| THURSDAY | | |
| FRIDAY | | |

THE WEEK'S
MOST
SIGNIFICANT
CONSOLATION

THE WEEK'S
MOST
SIGNIFICANT
DESOLATION

THE MOST
IMPORTANT
THING YOU
LEARNED THIS
WEEK

# ETERNITY

I believe God loved me into life and so I commit myself never to break relationship with anyone by taking from them what does not belong to me or even desire to do so!

| WEEK _____ | Write one word or phrase that brought you consolation today. Keep in mind joy because you are alive and loved - not because of "things" you possessed or did not possess. | OR: Write one word or phrase that brought you desolation today. Keep in mind sadness when you might have linked your self-worth to "things" you possessed or did not possess. |
|---|---|---|
| MONDAY | | |
| TUESDAY | | |
| WEDNESDAY | | |
| THURSDAY | | |
| FRIDAY | | |

THE WEEK'S
MOST
SIGNIFICANT
CONSOLATION

THE WEEK'S
MOST
SIGNIFICANT
DESOLATION

THE MOST
IMPORTANT
THING YOU
LEARNED THIS
WEEK

# ETERNITY

I believe God loved me into life and so I commit myself never to break relationship with anyone by taking from them what does not belong to me or even desire to do so!

| WEEK _____ | Write one word or phrase that brought you consolation today. Keep in mind joy because you are alive and loved<br>- not because of "things" you possessed or did not possess. | OR: Write one word or phrase that brought you desolation today. Keep in mind sadness when you might have linked your self-worth to "things" you possessed or did not possess. |
|---|---|---|
| MONDAY | | |
| TUESDAY | | |
| WEDNESDAY | | |
| THURSDAY | | |
| FRIDAY | | |

THE WEEK'S
MOST
SIGNIFICANT
CONSOLATION

THE WEEK'S
MOST
SIGNIFICANT
DESOLATION

THE MOST
IMPORTANT
THING YOU
LEARNED THIS
WEEK

# ETERNITY

I believe God loved me into life and so I commit myself never to break relationship with anyone by taking from them what does not belong to me or even desire to do so!

| WEEK _____ | Write one word or phrase that brought you consolation today. Keep in mind joy because you are alive and loved - not because of "things" you possessed or did not possess. | OR: Write one word or phrase that brought you desolation today. Keep in mind sadness when you might have linked your self-worth to "things" you possessed or did not possess. |
|---|---|---|
| MONDAY | | |
| TUESDAY | | |
| WEDNESDAY | | |
| THURSDAY | | |
| FRIDAY | | |

| | | |
|---|---|---|
| THE WEEK'S MOST SIGNIFICANT CONSOLATION | | |
| THE WEEK'S MOST SIGNIFICANT DESOLATION | | |
| THE MOST IMPORTANT THING YOU LEARNED THIS WEEK | | |

# ETERNITY

I believe God loved me into life and so I commit myself never to break relationship with anyone by taking from them what does not belong to me or even desire to do so!

| WEEK _____ | Write one word or phrase that brought you consolation today. Keep in mind joy because you are alive and loved – not because of "things" you possessed or did not possess. | OR: Write one word or phrase that brought you desolation today. Keep in mind sadness when you might have linked your self-worth to "things" you possessed or did not possess. |
| --- | --- | --- |
| MONDAY | | |
| TUESDAY | | |
| WEDNESDAY | | |
| THURSDAY | | |
| FRIDAY | | |

THE WEEK'S
MOST
SIGNIFICANT
CONSOLATION

THE WEEK'S
MOST
SIGNIFICANT
DESOLATION

THE MOST
IMPORTANT
THING YOU
LEARNED THIS
WEEK

# ETERNITY

I believe God loved me into life and so I commit myself never to break relationship with anyone by taking from them what does not belong to me or even desire to do so!

| WEEK _____ | Write one word or phrase that brought you consolation today. Keep in mind joy because you are alive and loved - not because of "things" you possessed or did not possess. | OR: Write one word or phrase that brought you desolation today. Keep in mind sadness when you might have linked your self-worth to "things" you possessed or did not possess. |
|---|---|---|
| MONDAY | | |
| TUESDAY | | |
| WEDNESDAY | | |
| THURSDAY | | |
| FRIDAY | | |

THE WEEK'S
MOST
SIGNIFICANT
CONSOLATION

THE WEEK'S
MOST
SIGNIFICANT
DESOLATION

THE MOST
IMPORTANT
THING YOU
LEARNED THIS
WEEK

# ETERNITY

I believe God loved me into life and so I commit myself never to break relationship with anyone by taking from them what does not belong to me or even desire to do so!

| WEEK _____ | Write one word or phrase that brought you consolation today. Keep in mind joy because you are alive and loved<br>- not because of "things" you possessed or did not possess. | OR: Write one word or phrase that brought you desolation today. Keep in mind sadness when you might have linked your self-worth to "things" you possessed or did not possess. |
|---|---|---|
| MONDAY | | |
| TUESDAY | | |
| WEDNESDAY | | |
| THURSDAY | | |
| FRIDAY | | |

| | | |
|---|---|---|
| THE WEEK'S MOST SIGNIFICANT CONSOLATION | | |
| THE WEEK'S MOST SIGNIFICANT DESOLATION | | |
| THE MOST IMPORTANT THING YOU LEARNED THIS WEEK | | |

# ETERNITY

I believe God loved me into life and so I commit myself never to break relationship with anyone by taking from them what does not belong to me or even desire to do so!

| WEEK _____ | Write one word or phrase that brought you consolation today. Keep in mind joy because you are alive and loved - not because of "things" you possessed or did not possess. | OR: Write one word or phrase that brought you desolation today. Keep in mind sadness when you might have linked your self-worth to "things" you possessed or did not possess. |
| --- | --- | --- |
| MONDAY | | |
| TUESDAY | | |
| WEDNESDAY | | |
| THURSDAY | | |
| FRIDAY | | |

THE WEEK'S
MOST
SIGNIFICANT
CONSOLATION

THE WEEK'S
MOST
SIGNIFICANT
DESOLATION

THE MOST
IMPORTANT
THING YOU
LEARNED THIS
WEEK

# ETERNITY

I believe God loved me into life and so I commit myself never to break relationship with anyone by taking from them what does not belong to me or even desire to do so!

| WEEK _____ | Write one word or phrase that brought you consolation today. Keep in mind joy because you are alive and loved - not because of "things" you possessed or did not possess. | OR: Write one word or phrase that brought you desolation today. Keep in mind sadness when you might have linked your self-worth to "things" you possessed or did not possess. |
|---|---|---|
| MONDAY | | |
| TUESDAY | | |
| WEDNESDAY | | |
| THURSDAY | | |
| FRIDAY | | |

THE WEEK'S
MOST
SIGNIFICANT
CONSOLATION

THE WEEK'S
MOST
SIGNIFICANT
DESOLATION

THE MOST
IMPORTANT
THING YOU
LEARNED THIS
WEEK

# ETERNITY

I believe God loved me into life and so I commit myself never to break relationship with anyone by taking from them what does not belong to me or even desire to do so!

| WEEK _____ | Write one word or phrase that brought you consolation today. Keep in mind joy because you are alive and loved - not because of "things" you possessed or did not possess. | OR: Write one word or phrase that brought you desolation today. Keep in mind sadness when you might have linked your self-worth to "things" you possessed or did not possess. |
|---|---|---|
| MONDAY | | |
| TUESDAY | | |
| WEDNESDAY | | |
| THURSDAY | | |
| FRIDAY | | |

|  |  |  |
|---|---|---|
| THE WEEK'S MOST SIGNIFICANT CONSOLATION | | |
| THE WEEK'S MOST SIGNIFICANT DESOLATION | | |
| THE MOST IMPORTANT THING YOU LEARNED THIS WEEK | | |

# ETERNITY

I believe God loved me into life and so I commit myself never to break relationship with anyone by taking from them what does not belong to me or even desire to do so!

| WEEK _____ | Write one word or phrase that brought you consolation today. Keep in mind joy because you are alive and loved - not because of "things" you possessed or did not possess. | OR: Write one word or phrase that brought you desolation today. Keep in mind sadness when you might have linked your self-worth to "things" you possessed or did not possess. |
|---|---|---|
| MONDAY | | |
| TUESDAY | | |
| WEDNESDAY | | |
| THURSDAY | | |
| FRIDAY | | |

THE WEEK'S
MOST
SIGNIFICANT
CONSOLATION

THE WEEK'S
MOST
SIGNIFICANT
DESOLATION

THE MOST
IMPORTANT
THING YOU
LEARNED THIS
WEEK

# ETERNITY

I believe God loved me into life and so I commit myself never to break relationship with anyone by taking from them what does not belong to me or even desire to do so!

| WEEK _____ | Write one word or phrase that brought you consolation today. Keep in mind joy because you are alive and loved - not because of "things" you possessed or did not possess. | OR: Write one word or phrase that brought you desolation today. Keep in mind sadness when you might have linked your self-worth to "things" you possessed or did not possess. |
|---|---|---|
| MONDAY | | |
| TUESDAY | | |
| WEDNESDAY | | |
| THURSDAY | | |
| FRIDAY | | |

| | | |
|---|---|---|
| THE WEEK'S MOST SIGNIFICANT CONSOLATION | | |
| THE WEEK'S MOST SIGNIFICANT DESOLATION | | |
| THE MOST IMPORTANT THING YOU LEARNED THIS WEEK | | |

# ETERNITY

I believe God loved me into life and so I commit myself never to break relationship with anyone by taking from them what does not belong to me or even desire to do so!

| WEEK _____ | Write one word or phrase that brought you consolation today. Keep in mind joy because you are alive and loved - not because of "things" you possessed or did not possess. | OR: Write one word or phrase that brought you desolation today. Keep in mind sadness when you might have linked your self-worth to "things" you possessed or did not possess. |
|---|---|---|
| MONDAY | | |
| TUESDAY | | |
| WEDNESDAY | | |
| THURSDAY | | |
| FRIDAY | | |

| | | |
|---|---|---|
| THE WEEK'S MOST SIGNIFICANT CONSOLATION | | |
| THE WEEK'S MOST SIGNIFICANT DESOLATION | | |
| THE MOST IMPORTANT THING YOU LEARNED THIS WEEK | | |

# ETERNITY

I believe God loved me into life and so I commit myself never to break relationship with anyone by taking from them what does not belong to me or even desire to do so!

| WEEK _____ | Write one word or phrase that brought you consolation today. Keep in mind joy because you are alive and loved - not because of "things" you possessed or did not possess. | OR: Write one word or phrase that brought you desolation today. Keep in mind sadness when you might have linked your self-worth to "things" you possessed or did not possess. |
|---|---|---|
| MONDAY | | |
| TUESDAY | | |
| WEDNESDAY | | |
| THURSDAY | | |
| FRIDAY | | |

THE WEEK'S
MOST
SIGNIFICANT
CONSOLATION

THE WEEK'S
MOST
SIGNIFICANT
DESOLATION

THE MOST
IMPORTANT
THING YOU
LEARNED THIS
WEEK

# ETERNITY

I believe God loved me into life and so I commit myself never to break relationship with anyone by taking from them what does not belong to me or even desire to do so!

| WEEK _____ | Write one word or phrase that brought you consolation today. Keep in mind joy because you are alive and loved - not because of "things" you possessed or did not possess. | OR: Write one word or phrase that brought you desolation today. Keep in mind sadness when you might have linked your self-worth to "things" you possessed or did not possess. |
|---|---|---|
| MONDAY | | |
| TUESDAY | | |
| WEDNESDAY | | |
| THURSDAY | | |
| FRIDAY | | |

THE WEEK'S
MOST
SIGNIFICANT
CONSOLATION

THE WEEK'S
MOST
SIGNIFICANT
DESOLATION

THE MOST
IMPORTANT
THING YOU
LEARNED THIS
WEEK

# ETERNITY

I believe God loved me into life and so I commit myself never to break relationship with anyone by taking from them what does not belong to me or even desire to do so!

| WEEK _____ | Write one word or phrase that brought you consolation today. Keep in mind joy because you are alive and loved<br>- not because of "things" you possessed or did not possess. | OR: Write one word or phrase that brought you desolation today. Keep in mind sadness when you might have linked your self-worth to "things" you possessed or did not possess. |
|---|---|---|
| MONDAY | | |
| TUESDAY | | |
| WEDNESDAY | | |
| THURSDAY | | |
| FRIDAY | | |

THE WEEK'S
MOST
SIGNIFICANT
CONSOLATION

THE WEEK'S
MOST
SIGNIFICANT
DESOLATION

THE MOST
IMPORTANT
THING YOU
LEARNED THIS
WEEK

# ETERNITY

I believe God loved me into life and so I commit myself never to break relationship with anyone by taking from them what does not belong to me or even desire to do so!

| WEEK _____ | Write one word or phrase that brought you consolation today. Keep in mind joy because you are alive and loved – not because of "things" you possessed or did not possess. | OR: Write one word or phrase that brought you desolation today. Keep in mind sadness when you might have linked your self-worth to "things" you possessed or did not possess. |
| --- | --- | --- |
| MONDAY | | |
| TUESDAY | | |
| WEDNESDAY | | |
| THURSDAY | | |
| FRIDAY | | |

| | | |
|---|---|---|
| **THE WEEK'S MOST SIGNIFICANT CONSOLATION** | | |
| **THE WEEK'S MOST SIGNIFICANT DESOLATION** | | |
| **THE MOST IMPORTANT THING YOU LEARNED THIS WEEK** | | |

# ETERNITY

I believe God loved me into life and so I commit myself never to break relationship with anyone by taking from them what does not belong to me or even desire to do so!

| WEEK _____ | Write one word or phrase that brought you consolation today. Keep in mind joy because you are alive and loved - not because of "things" you possessed or did not possess. | OR: Write one word or phrase that brought you desolation today. Keep in mind sadness when you might have linked your self-worth to "things" you possessed or did not possess. |
|---|---|---|
| MONDAY | | |
| TUESDAY | | |
| WEDNESDAY | | |
| THURSDAY | | |
| FRIDAY | | |

| THE WEEK'S MOST SIGNIFICANT CONSOLATION | | |
| THE WEEK'S MOST SIGNIFICANT DESOLATION | | |
| THE MOST IMPORTANT THING YOU LEARNED THIS WEEK | | |

# ETERNITY

I believe God loved me into life and so I commit myself never to break relationship with anyone by taking from them what does not belong to me or even desire to do so!

| WEEK _____ | Write one word or phrase that brought you consolation today. Keep in mind joy because you are alive and loved - not because of "things" you possessed or did not possess. | OR: Write one word or phrase that brought you desolation today. Keep in mind sadness when you might have linked your self-worth to "things" you possessed or did not possess. |
|---|---|---|
| MONDAY | | |
| TUESDAY | | |
| WEDNESDAY | | |
| THURSDAY | | |
| FRIDAY | | |

| | | |
|---|---|---|
| THE WEEK'S MOST SIGNIFICANT CONSOLATION | | |
| THE WEEK'S MOST SIGNIFICANT DESOLATION | | |
| THE MOST IMPORTANT THING YOU LEARNED THIS WEEK | | |

# ETERNITY

I believe God loved me into life and so I commit myself never to break relationship with anyone by taking from them what does not belong to me or even desire to do so!

| WEEK _____ | Write one word or phrase that brought you consolation today. Keep in mind joy because you are alive and loved - not because of "things" you possessed or did not possess. | OR: Write one word or phrase that brought you desolation today. Keep in mind sadness when you might have linked your self-worth to "things" you possessed or did not possess. |
|---|---|---|
| MONDAY | | |
| TUESDAY | | |
| WEDNESDAY | | |
| THURSDAY | | |
| FRIDAY | | |

THE WEEK'S
MOST
SIGNIFICANT
CONSOLATION

THE WEEK'S
MOST
SIGNIFICANT
DESOLATION

THE MOST
IMPORTANT
THING YOU
LEARNED THIS
WEEK

# ETERNITY

I believe God loved me into life and so I commit myself never to break relationship with anyone by taking from them what does not belong to me or even desire to do so!

| WEEK _____ | Write one word or phrase that brought you consolation today. Keep in mind joy because you are alive and loved - not because of "things" you possessed or did not possess. | OR: Write one word or phrase that brought you desolation today. Keep in mind sadness when you might have linked your self-worth to "things" you possessed or did not possess. |
|---|---|---|
| MONDAY | | |
| TUESDAY | | |
| WEDNESDAY | | |
| THURSDAY | | |
| FRIDAY | | |

THE WEEK'S
MOST
SIGNIFICANT
CONSOLATION

THE WEEK'S
MOST
SIGNIFICANT
DESOLATION

THE MOST
IMPORTANT
THING YOU
LEARNED THIS
WEEK

# ETERNITY

I believe God loved me into life and so I commit myself never to break relationship with anyone by taking from them what does not belong to me or even desire to do so!

| WEEK _____ | Write one word or phrase that brought you consolation today. Keep in mind joy because you are alive and loved<br>- not because of "things" you possessed or did not possess. | OR: Write one word or phrase that brought you desolation today. Keep in mind sadness when you might have linked your self-worth to "things" you possessed or did not possess. |
|---|---|---|
| MONDAY | | |
| TUESDAY | | |
| WEDNESDAY | | |
| THURSDAY | | |
| FRIDAY | | |

THE WEEK'S MOST SIGNIFICANT CONSOLATION

THE WEEK'S MOST SIGNIFICANT DESOLATION

THE MOST IMPORTANT THING YOU LEARNED THIS WEEK

# ETERNITY

I believe God loved me into life and so I commit myself never to break relationship with anyone by taking from them what does not belong to me or even desire to do so!

| WEEK _____ | Write one word or phrase that brought you consolation today. Keep in mind joy because you are alive and loved – not because of "things" you possessed or did not possess. | OR: Write one word or phrase that brought you desolation today. Keep in mind sadness when you might have linked your self-worth to "things" you possessed or did not possess. |
|---|---|---|
| MONDAY | | |
| TUESDAY | | |
| WEDNESDAY | | |
| THURSDAY | | |
| FRIDAY | | |

THE WEEK'S
MOST
SIGNIFICANT
CONSOLATION

THE WEEK'S
MOST
SIGNIFICANT
DESOLATION

THE MOST
IMPORTANT
THING YOU
LEARNED THIS
WEEK

# ETERNITY

I believe God loved me into life and so I commit myself never to break relationship with anyone by taking from them what does not belong to me or even desire to do so!

| WEEK _____ | Write one word or phrase that brought you consolation today. Keep in mind joy because you are alive and loved<br>- not because of "things" you possessed or did not possess. | OR: Write one word or phrase that brought you desolation today. Keep in mind sadness when you might have linked your self-worth to "things" you possessed or did not possess. |
|---|---|---|
| MONDAY | | |
| TUESDAY | | |
| WEDNESDAY | | |
| THURSDAY | | |
| FRIDAY | | |

THE WEEK'S
MOST
SIGNIFICANT
CONSOLATION

THE WEEK'S
MOST
SIGNIFICANT
DESOLATION

THE MOST
IMPORTANT
THING YOU
LEARNED THIS
WEEK

# ETERNITY

I believe God loved me into life and so I commit myself never to break relationship with anyone by taking from them what does not belong to me or even desire to do so!

| WEEK _____ | Write one word or phrase that brought you consolation today. Keep in mind joy because you are alive and loved - not because of "things" you possessed or did not possess. | OR: Write one word or phrase that brought you desolation today. Keep in mind sadness when you might have linked your self-worth to "things" you possessed or did not possess. |
|---|---|---|
| MONDAY | | |
| TUESDAY | | |
| WEDNESDAY | | |
| THURSDAY | | |
| FRIDAY | | |

THE WEEK'S
MOST
SIGNIFICANT
CONSOLATION

THE WEEK'S
MOST
SIGNIFICANT
DESOLATION

THE MOST
IMPORTANT
THING YOU
LEARNED THIS
WEEK

# ETERNITY

I believe God loved me into life and so I commit myself never to break relationship with anyone by taking from them what does not belong to me or even desire to do so!

| WEEK _____ | Write one word or phrase that brought you consolation today. Keep in mind joy because you are alive and loved - not because of "things" you possessed or did not possess. | OR: Write one word or phrase that brought you desolation today. Keep in mind sadness when you might have linked your self-worth to "things" you possessed or did not possess. |
|---|---|---|
| MONDAY | | |
| TUESDAY | | |
| WEDNESDAY | | |
| THURSDAY | | |
| FRIDAY | | |

| | | |
|---|---|---|
| THE WEEK'S MOST SIGNIFICANT CONSOLATION | | |
| THE WEEK'S MOST SIGNIFICANT DESOLATION | | |
| THE MOST IMPORTANT THING YOU LEARNED THIS WEEK | | |

# ETERNITY

I believe God loved me into life and so I commit myself never to break relationship with anyone by taking from them what does not belong to me or even desire to do so!

| WEEK _____ | Write one word or phrase that brought you consolation today. Keep in mind joy because you are alive and loved - not because of "things" you possessed or did not possess. | OR: Write one word or phrase that brought you desolation today. Keep in mind sadness when you might have linked your self-worth to "things" you possessed or did not possess. |
|---|---|---|
| MONDAY | | |
| TUESDAY | | |
| WEDNESDAY | | |
| THURSDAY | | |
| FRIDAY | | |

| | | |
|---|---|---|
| THE WEEK'S MOST SIGNIFICANT CONSOLATION | | |
| THE WEEK'S MOST SIGNIFICANT DESOLATION | | |
| THE MOST IMPORTANT THING YOU LEARNED THIS WEEK | | |

# ETERNITY

I believe God loved me into life and so I commit myself never to break relationship with anyone by taking from them what does not belong to me or even desire to do so!

| WEEK _____ | Write one word or phrase that brought you consolation today. Keep in mind joy because you are alive and loved - not because of "things" you possessed or did not possess. | OR: Write one word or phrase that brought you desolation today. Keep in mind sadness when you might have linked your self-worth to "things" you possessed or did not possess. |
|---|---|---|
| MONDAY | | |
| TUESDAY | | |
| WEDNESDAY | | |
| THURSDAY | | |
| FRIDAY | | |

| THE WEEK'S MOST SIGNIFICANT CONSOLATION | | |
|---|---|---|
| THE WEEK'S MOST SIGNIFICANT DESOLATION | | |
| THE MOST IMPORTANT THING YOU LEARNED THIS WEEK | | |

# Sacred Story Institute
Ignatian Spirituality for Third Millennium Evangelization

1401 E Jefferson, Suite 405
Seattle, WA 98122
sacredstory.net

Made in the USA
Monee, IL
28 July 2023

40005494R00063